GALATIANS WITHOUT TEARS

William J. Dalton, S.J.

GALATIANS
WITHOUT TEARS

A Liturgical Press Book

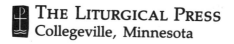

THE LITURGICAL PRESS
Collegeville, Minnesota

Cover illustration: Glass window from Sacred Heart Church, Yea, Australia
Cover design and photo: Bruno Colombari, S.S.P.

First published in 1992 by St. Paul Publications, Homebush, Australia.
Copyright © William Dalton, S.J., 1992. This edition for the United States
of America and Canada published by The Liturgical Press, Collegeville, Minnesota. Printed in the United States of America.

1	2	3	4	5	6	7	8	9

Library of Congress Cataloging-in-Publication Data

Dalton, William J. (William Joseph)
    Galatians without tears / William J. Dalton.
      p. cm.
    ISBN 0-8146-2227-5
    1. Bible. N.T. Galatians—Criticism, interpretation, etc.
I. Title.
BS2685.3.D355 1992   93-18782
227'.406—dc20   CIP

CONTENTS

FOREWORD

The title of this small work is meant to represent two things: first, an effort to make this famous letter of Paul more comprehensible to the student and the general reader, less frustrating and so less 'tearful', and second a sincere desire to remove the scandal which provoked so many Jewish tears in the past. Galatians, in its common Christian interpretation, has provided over the centuries the strongest ground for the 'teaching of contempt'. One only has to reflect how the words of Gal 4:30 have been applied to the Jews: 'Drive out the slave and her son, for the son of the slave shall not share the inheritance with the son of the free woman.' Christians, in earlier times, have been only too diligent in 'driving out' the Jews and, in more modern times, they showed little concern when the brutal command, 'H'raus Juden,' was the prelude to the extermination of millions of Jews in concentration camps.

This study is presented as a modest contribution to a comparatively new line of discussion about Paul and Israel. It makes no attempt to solve all the problems or to present all the learned documentation of a full-scale commentary. Sometimes there is value in offering an interpretation of a biblical book without too many complications, in the hope that the reader may be able to arrive at a vision of the whole text. Scholarly development usually begins with an intuition of meaning, which then, of course, has to be justified by detailed and learned examination. In this work we have only a beginning: much work remains to be done.

The introduction aims at providing those elements of background necessary for the right understanding of Paul's letter to the Galatians. This is followed by a translation and commentary which incorporate the ideas found in the introduction. The introduction avoids footnotes, but, from time to time, provides short bibliographies which may help the reader to follow up some point of interest. Few of the better known exegetical works will be listed here, since most of them follow the well-worn path which I am rejecting. Nor have I any desire, at the moment, to enter into a general debate on the subject. The short commentary on the text is not meant to provide a full exegetical treatment, but only an elucidation of those points which need to be clarified for a basic understanding of the letter.

INTRODUCTION

1 | PAUL AMONG JEWS AND GENTILES

This work is presented as part of a new approach to Paul's letter to the Galatians which goes very much against the prevalent and long established line of Pauline exegesis. It is the fruit of many years given to the teaching of Paul, particularly the letters to the Galatians and the Romans, to students at various levels. Paul is so often presented in commentaries old and new as a writer who seems to take almost a perverse pleasure in disguising his meaning.

Yet Paul is a powerful, intelligent and attractive writer. A sympathetic reader senses that he does have a clear and consistent message. Hence the impression that there is something radically wrong with the accepted approach to Galatians (and, for that matter, to Romans, which we are not directly concerned with here). To my mind, much of the problem lies in the fact that the prevalent understanding of Galatians is based on a number of presuppositions which need challenging. One such presupposition has made Galatians into a timeless statement of theology largely dominated by the controversies of the reformation:

the Judaisers who insist on the Law for justification (and behind them Judaism) really stand for the Roman Catholics with their emphasis on good works. Thus Galatians is seen as the great charter of liberty, in which faith and grace are set over against a barren legalism, that of the Judaisers and the Jews and also, of course, of the Roman church. The influence of this tradition is still seen in many Protestant exegetical works. Commentators see the doctrine of justification by faith and not by works as Paul's great contribution to Christian theology. Some would say that in Galatians we have the ageless contrast between religion and faith. Roman Catholic scholars may make a number of adjustments to suit their own tradition, but, by and large, they see in justification by faith an important element in Pauline theology. But, whatever the merit of such theological constructs, the question can be well asked whether in fact they are grounded on Paul's own gospel and not on a misunderstanding of it.

Another presupposition, connected with the above, is the image of Judaism at the time of Paul as a barren and pedantic system, a religion of the letter, but without the Spirit, and unworthy successor to the vital faith of what Christians call the Old Testament. But in fact the Judaism which Paul knew was a dynamic and powerful religion, respected and even protected in the whole of the Roman Empire. There is evidence of a vigorous proselytising movement amongst Gentiles. So diaspora Jews were not a people confined to ghettos (which were a later Christian invention), but rather gave Paul serious competition in his quest to bring salvation to the pagan world.

To indicate Jewish-Gentile relationships in New Testament times we could start with a citation from Josephus, the renowned Jewish historian and apologist:

> The masses have long since shown a keen desire to adopt our religious observances, and there is not one city, Greek or barbarian, nor a single nation, to which our custom of abstinence from work on the seventh day and our prohibition in the matter of food is not observed (*Apion*, 2:282-284).

Josephus, it must be admitted, is a witness of dubious worth, but there is no reason to question the testimony of Philo, the great Alexandrian Jewish scholar of New Testament times:

> Not only Jews but every kind of people, particularly those who take more account of virtue, have so far grown in holiness as to value and honour our laws ... They attract and win the attention of all, of barbarians and Greeks, of dwellers on the mainland and islands, of nations of the east and of the west, of Europe and Asia, of the whole inhabited world from end to end (*Life of Moses*, 2:17-21).

In early rabbinic literature there appears no consistent Jewish attitude towards Gentiles. Pagans, who were circumcised and undertook to observe the Law were generally regarded as the equivalent of Jews. But what of other pagans? Christians might look at their own traditions to appreciate the variety of Jewish views. The teaching of the church has varied and still varies in its teaching about non-Christians. It was common enough in the past to damn them all to hell (and there are still numerous representatives of this pessimistic view in some sections of Christianity), while there are others who maintain that the love and power of God can reach out to save all human beings. A similar difference of views was found in rabbinical teaching. Some rabbis held that there could be righteous Gentiles. One famous rabbi, Akiba, is recorded as saying: 'Beloved is man for he was created in the image (of God); still greater was the love in that it was made

known to him that he was created in the image of God'
(*Sayings of the Fathers*, 3:14-15). The Jewish historian
Josephus (*Life*, 23), while he speaks of Jews who wanted
to force pagans to be circumcised, insists that, in his own
view, Gentiles should be allowed to worship God in the
way they saw fit. He also cites as part of the Mosaic Law:
'Let no one blaspheme those gods which other cities regard
as such' (*Antiquities*, 4.8.10).

Thus, while it is possible to find examples of Jewish
rejection of pagans and even of contempt, this was by
no means their general attitude. On the side of the pagans,
there was in New Testament times a wide-spread attrac-
tion, evidenced in pagan literature, towards the Jewish
religion. The recent work of M. Stern, *Greek and Latin
Authors on Judaism* (Vol 1-3: Jerusalem: The Israel Academy of Sciences and Humanities, 1976, 1980, 1988),
particularly the first volume, indicates to what degree the
pagan world was influenced by Judaism.

One has only to read through Stern's volume, *From
Herodotus to Plutarch*, to see how many pagan historians
knew about the Jews and treated them and their history
with some sympathy. They often misunderstand both the
history and customs of the Jews and, often enough there
are less friendly references, but it cannot be said that
there was a general attitude of hostility. The anti-Jewish
statements of well known Jewish writers, such as Seneca,
Juvenal and Tacitus, are not so much a token of a common anti-Jewish attitude among the pagans, but rather
an effort to stem the flow of Jewish influence and even
conversions to Judaism. The laws issued in Rome against
the circumcision (predominantly a Jewish religious rite)
of pagans indicates the extent of Jewish influence.

It is clear that there were numerous conversions of
Gentiles to Judaism during New Testament times. The

saying attributed to the great Hillel represented the view of many Jews: 'Be one of the disciples of Aaron a lover of peace, following after peace, loving mankind and drawing them to the Law' (*Sayings of the Fathers*, 1.12). It follows that there was a missionary attitude among a good number of Jews. We have no evidence for an organised mission aimed at gaining proselytes, but there is no doubt that many Jews saw it as part of their religious vocation to spread their 'good news' among the pagans. Pagan witnesses point in the same direction. Thus the historian Valerius Maximus mentions the expulsion from Rome of over-zealous Jews: 'The same Hispalus banished the Jews from Rome, because they attempted to transmit their sacred rites to the Romans (Stern, *Greek and Latin Authors*, I, 358). Horace writes (*Sermones* I, 4:142-143), 'We, like the Jews, will compel you to make one of our throng.' Seneca is cited by Augustine (*De Civitate Dei*, VI, 11, 'De Superstitione') as saying, 'Meantime the customs of this accursed race have gained such influence that they are now received through all the world. The vanquished have given laws to the victors.' Circumcision, which was by far a predominantly Jewish custom, was so widespread among pagans in Rome that laws were issued forbidding it. All this is borne out by the words of Jesus in Mt 32:15, 'Alas for you, scribes and Pharisees, you hypocrites! You travel over sea and land to make a single proselyte, and anyone who becomes one you make twice as fit for hell as you are.' The note on this text in *The New Jerusalem Bible* (p.1647) reflects the general view of the scholarly world, 'Jewish propaganda was extremely active in the Greco-Roman world.'

I think that we may take it as a reasonable hypothesis that Paul's interest in the salvation of the Gentiles did not begin when he met the risen Lord. In Gal 5:11, he mentions that in former times he did preach circumcision. He writes, 'But if, brothers, I am still preaching circumcision *(peritomén eti kéryssó)*, why am I still being persecuted?' The Greek verb *kéryssó* is elsewhere used by Paul for his preaching of the Christian gospel. The noun *peritomé* literally refers 'circumcision', but this meaning is commonly extended to include the whole Jewish religion. Paul is alluding to an activity which had some similarity to his later preaching of the Christian gospel. This surely means that, as a Jew, he proclaimed to pagans the necessity of circumcision for salvation. It is hardly likely that Paul insisted at the beginning of his Christian mission on the circumcision of his Christian converts, but, having had little success with this presentation of the Christian faith, he changed later to proclaim a Torah-free gospel. On the other hand, before his conversion, Paul could well have taken part in Jewish missionary activity among the Gentiles and insisted on the strict line that pagans would have to become Jews by circumcision in order to arrive at salvation.

It was of such Jewish missionaries that Paul was probably thinking in his sarcastic remarks on Jews in Rom 2:17-24:

> But if you call yourself a Jew and rely upon the law and boast of your relation with God and know his will and approve what is excellent, because you are instructed in the law, and if you are sure that you are a light to the blind, a light to those in darkness, a corrector of the foolish, a teacher of children, having in the law the embodiment of knowledge and truth ...

Behind all Paul's problems with the Jews of his time lay their refusal to accept his own call to be a light to the Gentiles. According to Paul, in rejecting his Torah-free mission to the pagans, the diaspora Jews were disobedient to the God who had called them to be 'a light to the nations, that my salvation may reach to the end of the earth' (Is 49:6). In 1 Thess 2:14-16 Paul's anger breaks out against his Jewish contemporaries precisely because they 'hinder us from speaking to the Gentiles that they may be saved'.

It must be admitted that the view presented above has not gone without challenge. In a recent article, 'A First-Century Jewish Mission to Christians?' published in *Pacifica* 5 (1992) pp. 32-42 ..., Jerome Murphy-O'Connor presents quite another picture of Jewish-Christian relationships. He denies that Paul was ever, before his meeting with the risen Lord, engaged in missionary activity to convert pagans to Judaism, he questions the very existence of religious Gentile God-fearers. He sees this approach as part of a 'revisionist trend' a view which would make Paul believe that Christ was irrelevant for Jews, for whom the Law remained a valid means of salvation.

The last point is a very serious accusation: it would deny the universal nature of the Christian religion. The problem here is that Paul did not formulate a gospel directed to the conversion of Jews. It is eminently clear from his own writings that he was sent to preach to the Gentiles. But it is equally clear that Paul had a very high regard for the church at Jerusalem, which was engaged in a missionary effort directed to Jews. Unlike Paul's converts, the church at Jerusalem did not find observance of the Mosaic Law incompatible with the Christian gospel. Murphy-O'Connor names a work of Gaston as representative of the 'revisionist trend' he repudiates (p. 32), but this same author dedicates a whole chapter, 'Paul and Jerusalem' (pp. 107-115), to discuss Paul's approval of the Christian mission to the Jews and to indicate what form this gospel may have taken. Paul is hardly presented as regarding Christ as irrelevant to Jews.

Murphy-O'Connor sums up Jewish-Christian relationships in biblical times as follows: 'Jewish attitudes ranged between the extremes of forced conversion to Judaism with the imposition of circumcision and a profoundly patronising contempt of Gentiles. Inevitably the Greco-Roman world reciprocated in kind throughout the same scale' (p. 35). No place here for the Jewish teaching on 'the righteous Gentile', the broader views of a Hillel or an Akiba, and on the pagan side no place for the picture given by Philo of Gentiles who 'have grown so far in holiness as to value and honour our laws' or for the centurion who loved the Jewish people (Lk 7:5). On this last text, *The New Jerusalem Bible* has this note: 'Evidently a gentile in sympathy with Judaism, like Cornelius, Acts 10:1-2a.'

In the consideration of Jewish-Gentile relationships, the chief element adduced by Murphy-O'Connor is the special political and social situation of the Jews. It is true that the Jews showed such dedication to what they regarded as the law of God and were so numerous that Roman authorities were forced to grant them privileges, particularly with regard to the sabbath and military service. These privileges, which Murphy-O'Connor calls 'this iniquitous situation' (p. 37), no doubt led to considerable anti-Jewish feeling. While, admittedly, this is an important element to be considered, it is only one part of the story. How explain the Roman legislation against the circumcision of pagans or the considerable number of pagans, some of them of high standing, who were converted to Judaism? If the only influence exercised by the Jews was political pressure to ensure the continuation of their privileges, then Murphy-O'Connor is justified in interpreting the texts cited above from Horace and Seneca along these lines; but the same author writes (p. 39), 'Diaspora Judaism was missionary in fact if not in intention. If it did not seek out converts, it nonetheless attracted them by their quality of its religious life.' This picture hardly fits in with the universal mutual hostility between Gentiles and Jews given earlier by the same author.

It is hard to believe that diaspora Judaism was missionary in fact only, with the Jews being completely passive towards the acquisition of converts among the pagans. Mt 23:15 is a clear witness to active proselytising of pagans: to explain the text in any other way seems to be special pleading.

We also have the saying attributed to Hillel about 'drawing them (the Gentiles) to the Law,' cited above. Murphy-O'Connor himself gives an account (p. 33) of the case related in Josephus of King Izates of Adiabene 'converted not by a missionary but by a Jewish merchant named Ananias'. This would seem to be a good example of what was generally going on: a widespread missionary attitude among devout Jews. We have no evidence, it is true, of Jews dedicated solely to the preaching of Judaism to the pagans, although there may well have been such a group. It would be going beyond the evidence to claim that Paul had been a Jewish missionary in exactly the same way as he was later a preacher of the Christian gospel. But, whatever course his life took before his meeting with the Christian movement, it is quite likely, in the light of Gal 5:11, that, when occasion offered, he 'preached circumcision' to the Gentiles.

Murphy-O'Connor explains Gal 5:11 in the setting of a dispute among Jews whether circumcision was necessary for pagans who were converted to the Jewish faith. Paul thus 'preached circumcision' to his fellow Jews in insisting that proselytes should be circumcised. This interpretation seems less likely: it does less justice to the text, in particular to the verb *kéryssó*, 'preach', used elsewhere by Paul of his proclamation of the Christian gospel. In addition it supposes that this dispute was going on in Pauline circles: the insistence on circumcision for pagan converts to Judaism was by far the more common practice.

One might add that the question of Paul's proselytising among Gentiles before his conversion to Christianity is a secondary matter. If he was concerned about the salvation of Gentiles even before his meeting with the risen Jesus, it is easier to understand why he links so closely his call to be a Christian with his mission to the Gentiles (Gal 1:15). But this discussion does not touch my main argument, to be treated later, that Paul's Christian mission was to pagans only: this is founded on Paul's own authentic letters.

The vast majority of commentators accept in general the picture which Luke gives of pagans, commonly called 'God-fearers', who were sympathetic to Judaism as a religion and attached in varying degrees to the synagogue, but who, for obvious reasons, did not want to take the last step (in the case of men, circumcision) and to become proselytes. The note of *The New Jerusalem Bible* (1985) on 'God-fearing' in Acts 10:2 would represent by far the opinion of the majority of scholars: 'The expression "fearing God", 10:2,22,35; 13:16,26, and "worshipping God", 13:43,50; 16:14; 17:4,17; 18:7, are technical terms for admirers and followers of the Jewish religion who stop short of circumcision.' The presence of such pagans at the synagogue would help to explain why Paul seems to have constantly started with the synagogue in his mission to the Gentiles. Some scholars would go so far as to claim that most of Paul's converts belonged to this class.

It should be noted that there are some scholars who deny the existence of this class of Gentile. Their argument supposes that Luke's 'God-fearers' are 'a literary fiction invented by Luke to legitimise a Gentile church with Old Testament roots' (Murphy-O'Connor, 'A First-Century Jewish Mission to Gentiles?', p. 40). The main, in fact the only argument, is the absence of any clear reference to them in the numerous inscriptions from diaspora synagogues.

The argument from silence is always difficult to sustain, and in this case, it is upset by a recent inscription discovered at Aprodisias, in which a list of Jews and Gentiles is given, the latter being called *theosebeis*, the equivalent of 'God-fearers', a term applied on occasion to Jews themselves. This is a religious title and it is difficult to interpret it, as Murphy-O'Connor does (p. 41) as referring to Gentiles who gave financial assistance towards the maintenance of a soup-kitchen run by the Jews for the poor, possibly in order to get the Jewish vote. It is hard to believe that Jews would call such idol-worshipping pagans 'God-fearers'.

In any case, the argument that Luke invented the 'God-fearers' is difficult to accept. While Luke's sources did not always give him an exact picture of the social or religious scene at the time of Paul, he did surely know his own time and his readers could judge him by that. Besides the testimony of Luke, there is ample evidence of pagan 'God-fearers' in early Jewish literature (See Stern, *Greek and Latin Authors on Jews and Judaism*, Vol. 2, 102-107). All this is in perfect accord with the picture of the influence of Jews in the Roman Empire given above by Josephus and Philo. Thus, without going into all the ramifications of argument and counter-argument in the discussion (which is largely about words) I think it may be said that modern scholarly opinion still favours strongly the existence of God-fearers.

Another point worth mentioning is the need to explain how Paul's constant use of scripture could have been comprehensible to his newly converted pagan converts. A number of commentators find the explanation in the fact that many of these new Christians had formerly been God-fearers already educated in the Jewish scriptures.

Commentaries

It can be said that in all the commentaries on Galatians which I know it is supposed that Paul, in attacking the Judaisers, is, at least indirectly, attacking Judaism itself. This is true of the more recent learned commentaries: H.D. Betz, *Galatians* (Hermeneia; Philadelphia: Fortress Press, 1979); F.F. Bruce, *The Epistle to the Galatians* (The New International Greek Testament Commentary; Exeter: Paternoster and Grand Rapids: Eerdmans, 1982); R.Y.K. Fung, *The Epistle to the Galatians* (The New International Commentary on the New Testament; Grand Rapids: Eerdmans, 1988). See particularly Bruce, 202-203 and Fung, 191. In this latter reference Judaism, according to Paul in Galatians, is equated with paganism. Roman Catholic commentaries, including the recent popular but influential works: *The New Jerusalem Bible* (1985) and *The New Jerome Biblical Commentary* (1990) in their treatment of Galatians avoid such extreme statements, but follow the same general line: Paul is attacking not merely the Judaisers but Judaism itself. On the question of the God-fearers, see Stern, particularly for Jewish sources, *Greek and Latin Authors on Jews and Judaism*, Vol. 2, 102-107.

2 | A NEW APPROACH

A few modern scholars present quite a different interpretation of Galatians from that regularly proposed in commentaries. They see it as a letter set in a very particular situation with a limited and clearly defined purpose. First Paul himself, according to his own express and repeated statements, was sent by the Lord Jesus to proclaim the gospel to the Gentiles and to them only. Secondly, it is evident that the churches founded by Paul himself consist of converted Gentiles only. Thirdly, it is probable that Paul's adversaries, the so-called Judaisers, are not Jewish Christians but converted Gentiles.

Imagine the situation when Paul's letter was read out to the Galatian Christians: there was not a single Jewish Christian there, much less a Jew from the synagogue. We may take it that a good number of the hearers would have been former 'God-fearers', Gentiles associated to a greater or less degree with the synagogue. Thus when Paul uses terms such as 'under the Law' or 'works of the Law', he is thinking of the relation of the Mosaic

Law to pagans. At no point is he considering the relationship of Jews with the Law, whether these Jews be Christians or not.

Thus Paul is not dealing with the observance of the Law by the people of the covenant: in Jewish tradition covenant, Law and the scriptures were inseparable. His mission is to proclaim a Torah-free gospel to the pagans. Pagans do not stand within the covenant, and since they are not within the covenant by which Israel is saved, they find in the Law only a code which condemns. It is only for pagans that the Law is a prison, a temporary measure, a slavery from which Jesus Christ liberates those who have faith in him.

Some may find this relationship of pagans with the Mosaic Law strange and artificial. Yet behind Galatians there is the history of Jewish-Gentile relationships, in which, besides the commonly known anti-Semitism, there was also a strong proselytising movement, with constant discussions among the Jews themselves on how the Gentiles related with the Law. Thus Davies in *Paul and Rabbinic Judaism* can write (p. 66): 'We have recorded all the above details in order to show the reality of what we may call the Gentile Problem within Rabbinic Judaism and that it was "in the air" as it were in the Judaism of Paul's time.' This topic we shall discuss more fully in the section, 'The Torah and the Gentiles'.

If then we may assume that the relationship of Gentiles with the Law was a live issue in the time of Paul and that he himself had previously been involved in Jewish missionary activity among the Gentiles, then it makes sense to understand Paul's letter to the Galatians in this setting. Paul, after his meeting with the risen Lord, sees that his earlier belief, that Gentiles could be saved only by becoming members of the Jewish people, was misguided. While he continued to hold that Gentiles came under the condemnation of the Law, he now believed that they were to be saved, not by becoming Jews, but simply by faith in Jesus Christ. Even more, for pagans the two ways were incompatible: faith in Jesus excluded for them circumcision and observance of the Law. Because of his meeting with the risen Lord, Paul's interpretation of the Torah changed. While before he interpreted the Torah as requiring pagans to enter the covenant for salvation, now he saw in the same Torah a mandate to preach a Torah-free gospel to the pagans.

Paul simply does not touch the relationship of Jews, whether Christian or not, with the Law. As we have seen, this does not mean that for Paul 'Christ was irrelevant' for the Jews. For Paul the church at Jerusalem, where Christians could integrate observance of the Mosaic Law into their Christian faith, remained the centre of the Christian world, with which he was desperately anxious to remain in communion, and he fully approved of Peter's wider mission to the Jews (Gal 2:7-9).

When Paul speaks of himself, he is dealing with a special case: one called to give up the practice of the Law for the sake of his mission to the Gentiles. In all this there is a great deal of unfinished business. On the one hand, Paul, in Phil 3:4-11, seems to renounce his Judaism: the language in 3:7-8 could hardly be stronger. Yet he still regards himself as a Jew, coming under the jurisdiction of the synagogue and its punishments (2 Cor 11:24) and professing great love for 'his brothers, his kinsmen according to the flesh' (Rom 9:3).

It is beyond the scope of this work to deal with Rom 9-11 and Paul's mature reflections on the place of Israel in God's plan. It is however worth noting that Israel's 'disobedience' does not seem to be its rejection of the gospel, but its refusal to accept Paul's preaching to the Gentiles and his understanding that Gentile Christians, without observance of the Law, were equally with Israel the heirs of the patriarchal promises. It seems highly improbable that Paul, writing about C.E. 58, could simply say that Israel, as a whole, had rejected the Christian gospel. We have the evidence of Acts 21:20-21 of a flourishing Christian church of Law-observant Jews at Jerusalem. As for the diaspora Jews, it is most unlikely that Paul preached his Torah-free gospel to them (despite the presentation of Paul in Acts as a universal Christian missionary). The greatest settlement of Jews outside the Holy Land was at Alexandria: we have to presume a great deal to hold that they had been adequately evangelised by the time that Paul wrote Romans.

On the other hand, Paul had had actual experience of the bitter hostility of diaspora Jews towards his own mission to the Gentiles. In giving up personally the practice of the Law, he appeared to them a renegade Jew and, even more important, he was leading a rival religious movement against Jewish proselytisers to win the allegiance of the so-called God-fearers and other pagans. Paul understood his preaching of a Torah-free gospel to the pagans as being required as a fulfilment of the Torah itself. Thus Paul's disputes with the Jews of the diaspora were disputes about the interpretation of the Torah. Jews who would have formerly supported his work of proselytising among the pagans, violently opposed his gospel of freedom to these same pagans.

Reading

Pioneer works in this new approach are: W.D. Davies, *Paul and Rabbinic Judaism. Some Rabbinic Elements in Pauline Theology* (rev. ed., Harper Torchbooks; New York: Harper & Row, 1955). The first edition of this work was published as early as 1948 and its treatment of the relationship between Israel and the Gentiles (pp. 59-68) is particularly valuable. See also K. Stendahl, *Paul Among Jews and Gentiles* (Philadelphia: Fortress Press, 1976); J.G. Gager, *The Origins of Anti-Semitism* (New York/Oxford: Oxford University Press, 1985); L. Gaston, *Paul and the Torah* (Vancouver: University of British Columbia Press, 1987); P.M. van Buren, *A Theology of the Jewish-Christian Reality* (Vol. 1-3; San Francisco: Harper & Row, 1980, 1983, 1988); E.P. Sanders, *Paul and Palestinian Judaism* (London: SCM, 1977); M. Stern, *Greek and Latin Authors on Jews and Judaism* (Vol. 1-3; Jerusalem: The Israel Academy of Sciences and Humanities, 1976, 1980, 1988).

3 | PAUL AND ANTI-SEMITISM

In traditional Christian exegesis, Paul and particularly his letter to the Galatians, has provided an important support for the age-old anti-Jewish attitude, which has ranged from subtle, largely unconscious discrimination to open and even murderous violence. I have long known theoretically that God had bound himself irrevocably by his promises to the people of Israel, a view largely accepted by most theologically educated Christians of today. This came home to me very powerfully during three years I spent in Jerusalem, when I was privileged, on occasion, to join my Jewish friends in prayer in the synagogue.

Many authors maintain that Paul holds in Galatians that Judaism, from the time of Moses on, was never a religion of salvation. Israel, being under the Law, was without grace and faith and in fact, the equivalent of a pagan people. The Law was not given by God but by angels, demonic powers who kept Israel enslaved until the coming of Jesus. It would follow, of course, that those who did not become Christians would remain in this situation as slaves under the Law to sin.

Thus we have the desperate plight of a people lost in a hopeless legalism, professing to serve God, but actually worshipping a legal code and behind this code the demonic powers from which it came. In the background there lurks a capricious God, whom Israel all the time thought it was celebrating as Saviour and Lover. In fact, in this strange story, an unbiased onlooker might well conclude that Israel was more worthy of commendation than the God of Israel himself!

Thus, according to the common exegesis of Galatians (and Romans), Paul did well to celebrate the abrogation of the Law, the end of an era of slavery and curse which had plagued Israel from the time of Moses (Rom 10:4; Gal 4:24-31; 2 Cor 3:14). With the coming of Jesus the era of the lifeless letter was over and the era of the Spirit and of freedom had begun. It would follow that Israel, kept in bondage under the Law until the coming of Jesus, had no right to exist at all after this coming. Over the centuries, the Christian Church learnt and practised this 'teaching of contempt' only too well.

By a strange paradox, Paul retains the writings of this people, 'under the Law' and so without grace or faith, as divinely inspired and uses them continually to justify his theological arguments. It does not seem to occur to him (at least in Galatians) that these same scriptures bear incessant and unmistakable witness to a people perpetually loved by God, a people believing in him and, in spite of sin and wrong-doing, coming back to him in repentance to receive his reconciliation and pardon.

It can be said that the Judaism of Paul's day was corrupted by a lifeless legalism and that Paul read this back into the very nature of the Law. The evidence of modern research shows quite the contrary: the Judaism of Paul's time can in no way be justly described as a legalistic system. It was a dynamic and, to some degree, missionary religion, in which God was seen as the true source and goal of human life and in which there was no real danger of worshipping the Law in place of the Creator. In fact, the covenantal nomism of Judaism was not dissimilar from aspects of genuine Christian tradition.

While Paul must be judged by his own words and not by other New Testament writings, it is interesting to see how different is the religious world of Luke 1-2, where Zechariah, Elizabeth, Mary, Joseph, Simeon and Anna are commended for 'carrying out impeccably all the commandments and observances of the Lord' (Lk 1:6). Jesus himself said, 'The scribes and the Pharisees sit on Moses' seat; therefore do whatever they teach you and follow it …' (Mt 23:2) and 'Do not think that I have come to abolish the Law or the prophets; I have not come to abolish but to fulfil. For truly I tell you, until heaven and earth pass away, not one letter, not one stroke of a letter will pass from the Law until all is accomplished' (Mt 5:17-18). Hebrews 11 can celebrate the faith of the great heroes of Israel and include them in the 'great cloud of witnesses' (12:1). Even one who claimed to speak in the name of Paul in 2 Tim 1:5 could celebrate the faith of the mother and grandmother of Timothy, Paul's convert and 'loyal child in the faith' (1 Tim 1:2; cf. 2 Tim 3:14-15).

Such a rejection of Israel is not in keeping with the love which Paul professes for his own people elsewhere (Rom 9:1-5) nor with his express statement that God's calling of Israel and his gracious gifts to her are irrevocable (Rom 11:29). In Christian history, such texts did not suit the 'teaching of contempt' and were largely ignored or rationalised. The Christian church of today, whatever its past, has come to accept Jews as elder brothers and sisters under the God and Father of our Lord Jesus Christ. Hence there are good reasons for questioning an understanding of Paul which sets him at odds not only with himself but with the enlightened faith of the church of today.

It is not enough to say that Galatians represents only a stage in Paul's thinking, a stage which he largely re-voked in Romans. In its common interpretation Galatians, as read aloud in a Christian congregation today, represents an affront to truth and justice. And, despite the differ-ences, Romans, again in the common interpretation, shares to some degree in the same unfounded and pessimistic evaluation of Judaism. We are dealing with no less a mat-ter than the credibility of the Christian canon of scriptures.

Reading

It may be thought that the picture given above of the common interpretation of Galatians is exaggerated. Of course, there are differences of emphasis among scholars, but the basic line is the same. One highly praised work is that of H. Hübner, *Law in Paul's Thought* (Edinburgh: Clark, 1984). He writes (p. 24): 'The nomos is the product of angelic demonic powers.' 'The intention of the angelic Law is to drive men to sinful desires and so to disaster.' B.H. Brimsmead, in his *Galatians – Dia-logical Response to Opponents* (SBL Dissertation Series 65; Chico CA: Scholars Press, 1982) 121, presents even more sharply the same general line: 'However in Galatians grace has fallen com-pletely out of Israel's history and there is only a stark periodisa-tion: an era of law followed by an era of grace.' 'The Jews, from Moses to Christ, worshipped *hoi physei me ontes theoi*. Judaism and Paganism alike are nothing but "pre-Christian religion".'

For another approach see Gager, 197-264; Gaston, 15-34, 80-99, 135-150; van Buren, Vol. 2, 277-283; F. Müssner, *Tractate on the Jews* (Philadelphia: Fortress Press and London: SPCK, 1984) 135-153.

For a modern discussion of the whole problem of the interpretation of the New Testament in relation to Israel, see J.A. Charlesworth (ed.), *Jews and Christians: Exploring the Past, Present, and Future* (Shared Ground Among Jews and Christians. A Series of Explorations, Vol. I; New York: Crossroad, 1990).

4 | THE TORAH AND THE GENTILES

The interpretation of Galatians offered in this work presupposes a whole background of Gentile relationship with Israel rarely developed in commentaries. Thus to some readers it would seem incredible that Paul's teaching on the Law in Galatians should be wholly concerned with the relationship between the Torah and the Gentiles. In their minds, Torah is concerned with Jews alone.

We have already seen that in New Testament times there is ample evidence of the religious influence of the Jews on the people with whom they lived. Among Jews there was a considerable variety of opinion upon the status of the pagans who observed Jewish customs and frequently attended synagogue services. There was a common belief that the Mosaic Law, revealed on Sinai and not in the Holy Land, was actually revealed to all the nations, while Israel was the only one to accept it. Jewish tradition spoke of God's voice thundering from Mt Sinai in seventy different languages to the nations of the world. Another tradition had the nations send scribes to Mt Ebal where the

Law was inscribed. Here they translated it into seventy different languages. Again there is the tradition of the 'angels of the nations' (Sir 17:17; Deut 32:8: Dan 10:13b) who were present at the giving of the Law and that the nations chose their gods from them (See Gaston, *Paul and the Torah*, 'Angels and Gentiles', 35-44). Such traditions form a theological construct to explain why the nations are to be condemned for not keeping the Law.

It is in the context of the Judaising problem that expressions such as 'under the Law' and 'works of the Law' are found in Paul. Both are pejorative in meaning and are opposed to the new way leading to salvation brought about by the saving act of Christ. Nowhere in Jewish writings is the phrase 'under the Law' used to describe the relationship to the Law to Jews. It is rather a technical phrase used by Paul to indicate, in the context of the Judaising problem, the situation of Gentiles.

The same can be said of the expression, 'works of the Law'. This phrase is not found in the main stream of Jewish literature, but only in a couple of cases in the Qumran writings. In Paul it is used in a polemical way which contrasts persons who do the works of the Law against those who live by faithfulness (see the later discussion of *pistis*). The former are not justified (Gal 2:16), they are under a curse (Gal 3:10). They are without grace and outside the salvation of God. I find it difficult to apply this to the normal religious Jew of Paul's time.

Some authors soften the blow by interpreting 'works of the Law' as a 'nomistic way of life', emphasising the exclusive nature of the Jewish faith, which separated Jews rigidly from Gentiles, as, for example, in J.D.G. Dunn, *Romans 1-8*. (Word Bible Commentary 38a, Dallas, Texas: Word Books, 1988) 153-155. We always have this problem of apparent 'religious imperialism' with any religion which regards itself as 'true'. Whatever of this interpretation, the same charge could be brought against most of the New Testament, which often saw nothing but darkness and perdition in the pagan world: Paul's prayer for Christians is 'that you may be blameless and innocent, children of God without blemish in the midst of a crooked and perverse generation' (Phil 2:15; see Rom 1:18-31). And both the early church and contemporary Judaism were missionary in spirit, holding out hope to the pagans if they were prepared to be converted. On the whole, Judaism was as tolerant of non-Jews as the early Christian church was of non-Christians.

If the more common meaning of 'works of the Law' is taken, then we have the problem that the Jews of Paul's time are presented as people who thought they could buy their way into salvation by the practices of the Mosaic Law. But more recent research, such as that of Sanders, has shown that there is no evidence that the Judaism of Paul's day had such a perverted view of religion.

The solution to this problem (which is still not without its difficulties) would seem to be a return to the basic situation of Galatians (and Romans): Paul is writing to Gentile converts and to them alone. We are in the context of the Judaisers, who were attempting to impose on Paul's converts selected practices of the Jewish Law, including circumcision, which they claimed to be necessary for the full Christian life and for salvation. These practices, to my mind, are the 'works of the Law' which for Gentiles are incompatible with Christian faith. The Jewish Christians who believed that they could integrate observance of the Law into their Christian life, such as the church at Jerusalem, were never attacked for this by

Paul. On the contrary, Jerusalem remained for Paul the centre of the universal church.

Thus in the stricter Jewish view, the nations who rejected the Law are still 'under the Law', and bound by it. They refuse to obey it and come under its condemnation. Gentiles could be saved only by becoming proselytes and entering into God's covenant with Israel. Paul seemed formerly to have shared this opinion: he admits that once he 'preached circumcision' (Gal 5:11).

It should be noted that there were more tolerant Jewish teachers who believed that pagans were called on to observe only the so-called Noachic laws to be saved. Such 'righteous Gentiles' could enter the kingdom of God.

This was the background, then, of Paul's religious life, first as a Jew at Tarsus and later as apostle to the Gentiles. First, no doubt, he was involved in proselytising activity, convinced that the pagans among whom he lived, including those he met at the synagogue, could be saved only by belonging formally to Israel. Thus, even before he met the risen Jesus, he was zealous for the conversion of the pagans. While his motives for persecuting the early church are not clear, we are given a hint in 1 Cor 1:23, where he speaks of the proclamation of the cross of Christ as being 'an offence to the Jews'.

Even after his becoming a Christian, Paul still believed that for pagans the Law was nothing but a condemnation, a curse; but now he saw that the way of salvation for them was not the way of Israel, but the way of a Torah-free gospel. The revelation of the risen Jesus had led Paul to have a radically different interpretation of the Torah itself: this was the basis of his continuous controversies with the Jews, which led to the punishment he received from Jewish authorities in the synagogues (2 Cor 11:24).

Thus in Galatians Paul is not concerned with the Jews, either those of the synagogue or those of the church. It was the task of Peter and his associates to proclaim the gospel to the Jews (Gal 2:7-9). Paul was not called either to share this work or to formulate a Christian theology which would incorporate for Jews the practice of the Law. He is concerned only with the salvation of pagans by offering them a Torah-free gospel. He ended up himself in an ambiguous position: as apostle to the Gentiles, he no longer observed the Law and seemed on occasion to have even abandoned the covenant (Phil 3:4-11). This is at least logical, for in the Jewish mind, covenant and Torah inevitably go together. Yet elsewhere he regarded himself as a Jew and a lover of Israel (Rom 9:1-5). But it is significant that nowhere in his letters does he ever advise other Jewish Christians not to observe the Law. He was even most concerned to keep in communion with the church at Jerusalem, which seemed to have no problem in integrating belief in Jesus with the strict observance of the Law (see Acts 21:20).

Paul saw in Israel a people still loved and chosen by God. He had no difficulty with the mission of Peter and others to bring Jews into the church by means of a gospel which involved Torah observance. Some modern writers seem to think that, for Paul, non-Christian Jews do not come under the saving work of God in Jesus, but are saved solely through God's covenant with Israel. This I regard as quite impossible for Paul, who clearly saw in Jesus the saviour of the whole human race, through whom the final aeon for the whole universe was initiated. But it still remains unclear how exactly Paul envisaged the destiny of Israel: 'All Israel will be saved ... From Sion will come the deliverer' (Rom 11:26). What Paul has left in obscurity we do well to leave in obscurity. We can only guess at a developed theology of salvation for Israel that he might have written.

Reading

Gager, 55-88; Stern, Vol. 1; W.A. Meeks, *The First Urban Christians. The Social World of the Apostle Paul* (New Haven and London: Yale University Press, 1983), 26-27, 168; Gaston, 35-44, 116-134; M. Barth, *Ephesians 1-3* (AB 34; Garden City, NY: Doubleday, 1974) 244-248. W.J. Dalton, 'Once More Paul Among Jews and Gentiles', *Pacifica* 4 (1991) 51-61. For Paul's attitude to Jewish Christians, see Gaston, 'Paul and Jerusalem', 107-115.

5 | THE FAITH (FIDELITY) OF JESUS CHRIST

A matter of some importance is the interpretation of *pistis Iésou Christou* when found in the text of Galatians. A good deal of scholarly work has been done recently on this point and there seems to be a growing agreement that *pistis Iésou Christou* could well mean the personal faithfulness or fidelity of Jesus, rather than the faith of Christians in Jesus. There is often an exegetical problem in interpreting the genitive case in the texts of the New Testament. For example, does 'the love of God' mean God's love for us or our love for God? Often the context makes the meaning clear, but some texts need further study, such as: 'The love of God has been poured into our hearts' (Rom 5:5). Scholars are agreed that here this text refers to God's love for us. A similar problem is to be found in interpreting the 'saving justice *(dikaiosyné)* of God'. This issue is particularly important, since the term *pistis* has a close affinity to *dikaiosyné*, which could be paraphrased 'God's fidelity to his promises'. Most scholars would agree that the primary meaning of the 'saving justice of God' in Paul is the relationship which God has to human beings. While *dikaiosyné* from the context can refer more directly to the human side of the relationship, in Pauline theology it is always the initiative of God which is understood as fundamental.

The first thing to note is that *pistis* of itself can mean 'faithfulness': 'What if some were unfaithful? Will their faithlessness nullify the faithfulness *(pistin)* of God?' (Rom 3:3). It can also mean the 'faith', of the Christian believer, the common current translation in most cases. In fact, it is the context which is to decide which meaning to follow. While, in Paul's theology, a person must have faith in order to accept the good news, it is of more fundamental importance to realise what the good news actually is: 'I am not ashamed of the gospel. It is the power of God for salvation to everyone who believes' (Rom 1:16). The gospel is the story of God's power, his grace, his saving justice, which bring to fulfilment God's promises through the free cooperation of Jesus Christ, a cooperation Paul calls 'obedience': 'For just as by the one man's disobedience the many were made sinners, so by the one man's obedience the many will be made righteous' (Rom 5:19). Paul elsewhere speaks of 'the obedience of faith' (Rom 1:5). So there would seem to be no difficulty in speaking of the faith or the faithfulness of Christ, that attitude of trusting obedience to the Father expressed in his death on the cross.

Yet there would seem historically to be two reasons which made this difficult. It was common teaching, at least in Catholic theology, that it was fitting that Christ, as a divine person, should be endowed in his human nature with the beatific vision, which ruled out the possibility of faith, which was proper rather for people in the process of redemption. The other tradition, to be found particularly in Protestant theology deriving from Luther, saw in 'justification by faith' as the foundation of Pauline (and Christian) theology. The great contrast was between the faith of the believing Christian and the works of the Law (commonly understood as a spurious attempt at gaining salvation merely by good deeds). With this emphasis in mind, it was natural to translate *pistis Iēsou Christou* as 'faith in Jesus Christ'. Apart from these traditional interpretations, it could also be added that the verb *pisteuein* is commonly used in Paul with the meaning of 'believe in Christ'.

The discussion of this topic is vast and cannot be adequately treated here. Two points may be made: First, it is difficult to see how 'believing in Christ' is to be separated from 'works'. Paul himself says that the only thing which matters is 'faith working through love' (Gal 5:6). In fact, in his general theology, Paul insists as much on good works as he does on faith. Believing, in fact, is something a person does. Even if the origin of faith is divine, God's initiative still has to be accepted by a human being. Any idea of faith being somehow created within the human being with no cooperation on the human side seems unintelligible. Thus the contrast of 'faith' and 'works' does not seem to be a helpful one. A brilliant expositor of Paul's theology wrote: 'For we are what he has made us, created in Christ Jesus for good works, which God prepared beforehand to be our way of life' (Eph 2:10). Thus both faith and good works are equally the products of both God and the Christian believer.

Secondly, from a historical point of view, it does not seem that Paul was concerned with the general problem of legalism. His was a more limited problem: Was it necessary for the salvation of his Gentile converts that they should observe at least some practices (including circumcision) of the Jewish Law? In his gospel to the Gentiles Paul was contrasting two systems: that of simply accepting the salvation offered by God through the redemption wrought by his Son, Jesus Christ, or of finding in the practices of the Law the necessary complement to this redemption. While Paul does insist that the Christian must believe in Christ, which is short-hand for the gospel, his basic emphasis is not on what human beings do, but what God does and what Christ does. It is the story of God's saving justice, in which Christ fulfilled the Father's promises by his obedience to death on the cross (Phil 2:8). If this presentation of Paul's theology is correct, then it is warranted to look again at the context in which *pistis* is found and to give it the meaning indicated by the context.

Let us take an example to illustrate the points made above. In Gal 3:22 Paul writes: 'But the scripture has imprisoned all things under sin, so that what was promised might be given on the ground of the *pistis* of Jesus Christ to those who believe.' In this text, there would be an unbearable tautology if *pistis* referred to the faith of the Christian believer. If *pistis* refers to Christ's fidelity in his act of redemption, we have an excellent sense which, in any case, fits better the context of Paul's thought. It is to be noted that, in the *New Revised Standard Version* 'the faith of Jesus Christ' is given as an alternative translation.

Even when *pistis* is used by itself, we should not simply suppose that it refers to the faith of a Christian. Gal 3:23 provides an example: 'Now before *pistis* came, we were imprisoned and guarded under the Law until *pistis* would be revealed.' Just before this Paul has referred twice

explicitly to the fact that Abraham believed (3:6-9), so
Paul hardly means that justifying human faith was never
in the world before the coming of the Christian gospel.
It would seem much more likely that the *pistis* referred
to in 3:23 is the enactment of God's fidelity, involving
the saving work of Jesus. It is this *pistis* which has been
revealed: it is the equivalent of the gospel.

It would seem then that whenever *pistis* is found in
Paul, we should be governed by the context, which would
often link the term with Christ or God and not to the
Christian believer.

To sum up: the contrast set up by Paul in Galatians
is not that between the faith and works of Christians (sup-
porting the Lutheran insistence that we are justified by
faith alone), but between the works of the Law undertaken by pagan Christians and the economy of salvation
established by the fidelity and obedience of Jesus. Paul
does not have a problem about faith and works in general
(in contrast to Luther): his attack is centred on pagan
Christians who nullify the saving fidelity and saving action
of Christ by their reliance on fulfilment of the works of
the Law as a principle of salvation. Paul does not seem
to have any clear distinction between faith as such and
works as such: both require human activity under the
grace and power of God. Faith is the first of these move-
ments and underpins all the rest: it is both human and
divine. What finally matters is that faith which works
through love (Gal 5:6) 'Works of the Law' is a technical
expression for practices of the Law undertaken by Gentiles and should not be extended to include good works
in any context.

A growing number of scholars have come to accept the
meaning of *pistis* proposed above. This already indicates

a considerable shift in the interpretation of Paul. It still remains true that a great number of studies and commentaries on Galatians, including modern ones, maintain the former understanding of justification by faith, proposing Paul as the great defender of Christian freedom against legalism, of faith against 'religion'. Such studies should be read critically to see what comes from the text of Paul and what is read into the text by later controversies.

Reading

M.D. Hooker, 'PISTIS CHRISTOU' *NTS* 35 (1990) 321-342 (see other works referred to in this article). The fullest treatment of this new interpretation is that of R.B. Hays, *The Faith of Jesus Christ* (Chico: Scholars Press, 1983).

6 | CIRCUMSTANCES OF WRITING

Scholars are divided as to what Christian community Galatians was directed. I have no intention here to go into the ramifications of the two views, the so-called North-Galatian and South-Galatian theories. The former would associate Galatians more closely with Romans and set it after Paul's visits to North Galatia narrated in Acts 16:6 and 18:23. The second view would see in the 'Galatians' addressed in the letter the communities evangelised by Paul and Barnabas in the so-called first missionary journey (Acts 13-14). Thus, in this hypothesis, Galatians could be regarded as the first letter ever written by Paul. It is probably impossible to find decisive evidence for either of the theories. Given the unreliability of Acts for much of Paul's life and also the close association of Galatians with Romans, the North-Galatian theory seems the more probable.

No great consequences flow from this for the interpretation of the letter, which provides itself the basic background for its interpretation. Without thanksgiving and without praise, Paul launches into the controversy. The Galatians are abandoning the genuine gospel preached by Paul for a pseudo-gospel: they are cutting themselves off thereby from God. Paul then narrates the story which bears on this controversy, that of his meeting with the Risen Lord, his vocation to proclaim the gospel to the Gentiles, his association with the church at Jerusalem, his acceptance by Peter and the leaders at Jerusalem as a genuine apostle sent to the Gentiles and, finally, his public rebuke of Peter at Antioch, when this latter, by his authority, was putting pressure on Gentile converts to follow Jewish eating customs, thus depriving them of the freedom from the Law proclaimed by Paul's gospel.

The long argumentation (2:15 – 4:31) and the exhortation (5:1 – 6:10) which follow reveal more fully the situation. Paul's Christian adversaries take on circumcision, but do not keep the Law themselves (6:13). They require from the Galatians that they observe selected parts of the Law after being circumcised (3:10; 5:3). Paul uses every kind of argument to exalt the way of grace and freedom, the way of the fidelity of Jesus Christ, as against the way of the Law, which was and is, for the Galatians, the way of cursing and slavery. In fact, by taking on circumcision and the Law they are regressing to the state of paganism they were in before conversion (4:3,9). Throughout the argument Paul constantly refers to his Galatians and himself as 'we'. Except for 2:15-16 Paul in these texts is identifying himself with his Gentile converts. He is saying nothing about his Jewish past or the past of his fellow Jews.

In the process of Paul's argument, we never hear the positive arguments offered by the Judaisers. To pagan converts they could have been quite formidable. After all, the central figure of their faith, Jesus, was circumcised and observed the Law (even though he may have, at times, radically interpreted it). That a Christian should share the religion of Jesus might seem too obvious for words. And the Hebrew scriptures themselves insist on the unbreakable bond between Israel and the Lord. In addition, the mother church at Jerusalem, at the centre of Christian tradition, saw no difficulty in incorporating the Law and its practices into their Christian faith. The Christian way could well have been understood as a development within Judaism. Finally, even modern exegetes are at a loss to explain why precisely Paul insisted on a Torah-free gospel to the pagans. The old view that the Law as practised by the Jews represented a legalism opposed to faith and grace has been solidly and effectively challenged. Nor is the purely pragmatic view that he considered a Torah-free gospel much more likely to succeed among pagans a satisfactory explanation. The fact is that Paul saw his own acceptance of Christ as Lord as bound indissolubly to his mission to preach a Torah-free gospel to the Gentiles. We do not know what was the result of Paul's letter in the Galatian community, but we do know that Paul's gospel won the day in Christian history.

Reading

Müssner, 143-146; B. Holmberg, *Paul and Power* (Philadelphia: Fortress Press, 1978) 15-56. W.J. Dalton, ' "We" in Galatians,' *ABR* 38 (1990) 33-44.

7 | STRUCTURE FOR GALATIANS

Betz has proposed a structure for Galatians based on Greco-Roman rhetoric and epistolography. This seems to me to be basically valid, even though I am not sure that the divisions of the letter derive so explicitly from this sophisticated literary background. After all, Paul is writing to convince his readers to give up a wrong way of acting and to return to that which he taught them. Behind his argument lies the question of the legitimacy of his own authority. Thus it is natural that, after the epistolary introduction (1:1-5), he should briefly state what the problem is (1:6-12) and then set the record straight about the story of his own coming to the Christian faith, his vocation as apostle to the Gentiles, his relationship with the church at Jerusalem, his acceptance by the Jerusalem leaders as apostle to the Gentiles on the terms of a Torah-free gospel, and finally his open rebuke of Peter at Antioch in the defence of such a gospel and his rejection by Barnabas and the Jewish Christians at Antioch. It is by no means sure that even the Gentile Christians in the Antioch community stood with Paul in the dispute. Paul's silence on the outcome of the controversy implies rather that his rejection was total (1:13 – 2:14).

Now Paul's argument against his opponents begins in earnest, starting with a defence of his understanding of the gospel and of his role as apostle to the Gentiles (2:15-21). This is followed by a series of individual arguments to support his case, from Christian experience (3:1-5), from scripture (3:6-14), from legal custom (3:15-18); this is followed by a digression on the Law (3:19-25). Further proofs follow, from Christian tradition (3:26 – 4:11), from Paul's bond of friendship with the Galatians (4:12-20), from an allegorical understanding of scripture (4:21-31).

After the exposition of these arguments, there is a prolonged exhortation urging fidelity to Paul's gospel (5:1-12) and to the Christian way of life, the way of the Spirit (5:13 – 6:10). In the latter section he shows, against the claims of the Judaisers that, without the Law, the community would fall into moral anarchy, that the Spirit is more than sufficient to guide and strengthen the Galatian Christians in fulfilling the Law (5:13) in the Law of Christ (6:2), summed up in the commandment of love. The letter closes with a section in which Paul himself takes up the pen to make a final eloquent summary of the message of the whole letter (6:11-18).

All this can be schematically presented thus:

Epistolary introduction (1:1-5)

Paul's case in defence of his gospel (1:6—4:31)
Entrance into the argument (1:6-10)
The true story about Paul (1:11 – 2:14)
Paul's defence of his gospel (2:15-21)
Paul's argument in favour of his case (3:1 – 4:31)
  First proof from experience (3:1-5)
  Second proof from scripture (3:6-14)
  Third proof from legal practice (3:15-18)
  The law and the Gentiles (3:19-25)
  Fourth proof from Christian tradition (3:26 – 4:11)
  Fifth proof from friendship (4:12-20)
  Sixth proof from allegory (4:21-31)

Exhortation (5:1—6:10)

Epistolary conclusion (6:11-18)

THE LETTER
OF ST PAUL
TO THE
GALATIANS
A new translation

INTRODUCTION (1:1-5)

1 ¹ Paul, an apostle, not commissioned by human beings, nor by human authority, but by the authority
of Jesus Christ and of God the Father, who raised him
from the dead, ² and all the Christian believers who are
with me − to the churches of Galatia: ³ grace to you and
peace from God our Father and from the Lord Jesus
Christ. ⁴ It was Christ who gave himself up to take away
our sins and to rescue us from the present evil age, in
keeping with the will of our God and Father, ⁵ to whom
be glory for endless ages. Amen.

PAUL'S CASE IN DEFENCE OF HIS GOSPEL
(1:6 − 6:10)

Entrance into argument (1:6-10)

⁶ I am amazed that you have turned away so quickly from
him who called you by the grace of Christ and have taken
on another gospel. ⁷ Not that this is, in fact, another gospel
− it simply means that there are people who are disturbing you and trying to distort the gospel of Christ. ⁸ But
if anyone, even ourselves or an angel from heaven, preaches
to you a gospel contrary to the gospel we preached to you,
let such a person fall under the curse of God. ⁹ I now
repeat what I have already told you: If anyone proclaims
a gospel to you at variance with the gospel you have received,
let that person fall under the curse of God.

¹⁰ Do I give the impression that I am trying to persuade human beings? Or is it God I am intent on pleasing? Do you really think that I am concerned with win-
ning human favour? If I aimed at pleasing human beings,
I should not be the servant of Christ.

The true story about Paul (1:11 − 2:14)

[11] I want to make it quite clear to you, brothers and sisters, that the gospel which I proclaimed to you was not a human message. [12] I myself did not receive it from a human being; no person taught it to me. I received it through a revelation of Jesus Christ.

[13] You have surely heard how I lived in the past within Judaism: how I went to extremes in persecuting the church of God [14] and how I tried to destroy it, how, in the practice of Judaism, I outstripped most of my Jewish contemporaries in my boundless zeal for the traditions of my ancestors. [15] But when God, who had set me apart when I was still in my mother's womb and called me through his grace, chose [16] to reveal his son in me in order that I might proclaim him among the gentiles,*a* I did not confer with any human being, [17] nor did I go up to Jerusalem to see those who were apostles before me. On the contrary, I went off to Arabia, and later came back to Damascus.

[18] Three years later I did go up to Jerusalem to meet Cephas; I stayed with him fifteen days.*b* [19] But I did not

---

a Why did Paul, a dedicated Jew, see himself as sent to the gentiles, not to the Jews? It would seem that, even before his meeting with the risen Jesus, he was concerned with the salvation of the pagans (which was not uncommon with the Jews of his time). As a 'zealous' Jew, he probably belonged to the school of Shammai, which held that pagans must come under the covenant by circumcision to be saved. This would explain the mysterious reference of Paul in Gal 5:11 about his earlier preaching of circumcision. Through his meeting with the risen Lord, he understood that he was sent now to preach to the pagans, not circumcision, but a Torah-free gospel. He saw in this proclamation the fulfilment of the Torah itself.

b Note the contradictions between this account and that of Acts 9:26-30. Acts presents Paul as a universal preacher of the gospel, not set eyes on any other of the apostles, but I did meet James, the brother of the Lord. [20] Before God, I swear that what I am writing is the truth. [21] After this I went to the regions of Syria and Cilicia. [22] I was still unknown personally to the churches in Judaea which are in Christ. [23] The story they heard was simple, 'Our former persecutor is now preaching the faith he once tried to destroy,' [24] and they gave glory to God for me.

2 [1] It was fourteen years later that I went up to Jerusalem with Barnabas, taking Titus also with me. [2] The journey was due to a revelation I received.[c] I put before them − in private and with the people of standing − the gospel I preach among the gentiles, to ensure that the race I had run, and was running, should not be in vain. [3] Yet even then, they did not insist that my companion Titus, Greek though he was, should be circumcised − [4] this despite the efforts of certain sham-Christians, who had insinuated themselves into our company to spy on the freedom we have in Christ Jesus, intending to bring us into slavery. [5] But not for a moment did we give way to their demands; it was essential that the truth of the gospel be maintained for you.

one who proclaimed the gospel first to the Jews and, because the Jews rejected the message, then to the pagans. This is contrary to Paul's express testimony that he was sent only to the pagans. In fact, the evidence of all Paul's authentic letters is that the churches he founded were exclusively gentile in origin. This understanding of Paul's mission is basic to the interpretation of his letters, particularly Galatians and Romans.

c   This visit cannot be fully harmonised with that described in Acts 15:1-29. In particular, the compromise about food (15:20,29) seems to be a later development. Otherwise Paul would have no grounds for objecting to Peter's behaviour in Gal 2:11-14, in which he required of pagan converts conformity to Jewish food laws.

6 Those in the community regarded as important (I am not concerned about their real importance, since 'There is no favouritism with God'), these seemingly important people, I say, had nothing to add to my presentation. 7 On the contrary, they saw that the gospel for the uncircumcised had been entrusted to me, just as the gospel to the circumcised had been entrusted to Peter: 8 he who had given Peter the power to exercise his apostolate among the Jews, had given me the same power for my apostolate among the gentiles.*d* 9 Recognising the grace given to me, James, Cephas and John, people regarded as pillars of the community, offered their right hands to Barnabas and myself as a sign of partnership: we were to go to the gentiles, and they to the circumcised. 10 They had one request: that we should keep their poor in mind. This, in fact, was something I was already eager to do.

11 But when Cephas came to Antioch, I opposed him to his face, because he was clearly in the wrong. 12 Before certain people came from James, he used to take his meals with gentile Christians. But, after their arrival, he withdrew and began to keep apart, being afraid of the circumcised.*e* 13 The other Jewish Christians played the same

---

d It is clear that this division is not geographical, but personal. Paul's numerous references to his vocation indicate that he was sent to gentiles everywhere, not to Jews and gentiles in gentile lands, that is, outside of the Holy Land. There is no evidence that Paul ever preached the gospel to Jews. As we have seen, the testimony of Acts in this matter is to be disregarded.

e Peter's change could have been caused by regard for the Jewish Christians at Jerusalem. They were living in harmony with the Jewish authorities there precisely because they did observe the Law (cf. Acts 21:20-21). Their situation would have been precarious if it were known in Jerusalem that these 'people from James' had joined Peter in violating the Law in Antioch. Paul, intent on the freedom double game; even Barnabas was carried away and joined in their hypocrisy. [14] But when I saw that their behaviour did not square with the truth of the gospel, I said to Cephas in front of them all, 'If you, a Jew born and bred, live like the gentiles and not like the Jews, how can you insist that gentiles live like Jews?'

Paul's defence of his gospel (2:15-21)[f]

[15] We are Jews by birth and not gentile sinners. [16] Yet we know that no person is justified by the works of the Law,[g] but only through the fidelity of Jesus Christ.[h] So we have come to believe in Christ Jesus, in order that we might be justified by the fidelity of Christ and not by the works of the Law, for by the works of the Law 'no human being can be justified.'[i]

of the pagan converts, had little sympathy for Peter in this complicated situation. In a later, less controversial situation, he will be more flexible in making compromises about food (e.g. Rom 14).

f   This new section is probably not a continuation of Paul's address to Peter, but the beginning of his argument with the Galatians. 'We who are Jews by birth' would thus mean Paul and his Christian fellow missionaries among the pagans.

g   This is a technical phrase for works performed by pagans. For believing Jews, the Torah was never separated from the covenant, and was thus never just a code of works to be done: it was a way of faith and life in response to God's grace in bringing one into the covenant.

h   Or 'the faith of Jesus Christ'. Paul is not making the distinction between 'faith' and 'works' (as is normally supposed), but between the fidelity of Jesus to his Father's will (the basis of salvation) and the carrying out of certain precepts of the Law by pagans.

i   In this text Paul identifies himself with his pagan converts and his fellow workers who have adopted the pagan way of life. He would probably expect Peter, as one who, on occasion, had contact with pagan converts, to agree with him. But Peter, like other Jewish Christians, would see no problem in observing the Law, as God's will,

[17] But if we ourselves,[j] seeking to be justified in Christ, are discovered to be sinners,[k] does it follow that Christ is the agent of sin? Not at all! [18] If I now start rebuilding everything I once demolished,[l] then indeed I show myself a real transgressor. [19] For through the Law, I died to the Law,[m] in order to live to God. I share the crucifixion of Christ.[n] [20] The life I live now is not my life: it is life of Christ living in me. In my existence as a poor

within the framework of the Christian faith. It was common Jewish belief that salvation comes through God's mercy shown in the covenant, not through scrupulous observance of the Law. Thus Peter could agree with Paul that nobody is justified by following the Law merely as a code and also that justification comes from the fidelity of Jesus, who fulfilled the Law. Despite this agreement, his pastoral practice in his contacts with pagan converts could be quite different from that of Paul.

j   Paul is referring here to Jewish Christians, who, in company with himself, have given up the practice of the Law.

k   Like the pagans mentioned in 2:15, Paul insists that he and his fellow-workers among the pagans are necessarily obliged by this mission to violate the Law and so be sinners against the Law. With this neither Peter nor the church at Jerusalem would agree. Hence the rules drawn up in the 'council of Jerusalem' in Acts 15 for the common life of a mixed pagan-Jewish community, in which the traditional food laws of the Jews were to be observed.

l   Paul had insisted that the gentiles should be received into the church without observing the Law, and he himself had taken on this way of life. If he were now to insist on the observance of the Law for himself and for them, he would be indeed as transgressor (against the will of God).

m   Paul constantly cites the Torah to show that God calls the gentiles, through Christ, to salvation, without the observance of the Law. As apostles to the gentiles, in solidarity with them, he, in the name of the Torah, no longer observes the law as a code of behaviour. Thus, according to Paul, the Law as divine teaching and scripture is valid for all Christians; but its precepts regulating behaviour do not bind Gentiles.

n   The crucified Christ came under the curse of the Law as a code (3:13). See the comment on this verse.

human being, I have a new life through the fidelity of the Son of God who loved me and gave himself for me. ²¹ I do not set aside the grace of God. If indeed saving justice comes from the code of the Law, then Christ died in vain.*o*

Proofs of the argument (3:1 – 6:10)

Experience (3:1-5)

3 ¹ You stupid Galatians! Who has been putting a spell on you, the very people who have had presented before their very eyes Jesus Christ crucified? ² Would you please tell me one thing: Did you receive the Spirit by doing the works of the Law or by the preaching of the gospel?*p* ³ Can you be so stupid as to begin with the spirit and to end without the spirit?*q* ⁴ Have all your great experiences been in vain? Can this really be true? What do you say to this? ⁵ Does the God who gives you the Spirit and works miracles among you act in this way because you perform the works of the Law, or because of the preaching of (God's) fidelity?

Scripture (3:6-14)

⁶ Remember that Abraham 'put his faith in God, and this was reckoned to him as (God's) saving justice'.*r*

---

o No believing Jew would hold that saving justice came through the Law apart from the covenant. The problem came for gentile who, apart from the covenant, thought to find salvation through the practice of the Law as a code.

p Literally 'the proclamation of fidelity'. Here we are not dealing with the faith of the Christian, but with the proclamation and hearing of the gospel, the story of God's fidelity and saving justice.

q Paraphrase for 'with the flesh'.

r In the Hebrew of Gen 15:6, it was Abraham who reckoned his faith as the product of God's fidelity or saving justice. In the following

[7] You can be sure then that it is the people of (God's) fidelity who are children of Abraham. [8] Scripture, foreseeing that God would justify the gentiles through his fidelity,[s] declared the gospel to Abraham beforehand: 'In you all nations will be blessed.' [9] Thus it is that people of (God's) fidelity share the blessing with Abraham, the man of faith.[t]

[10] On the other hand, those who rely on the works of the Law are under a curse,[u] for scripture says: 'Cursed be all who do not abide by everything written in the book of the Law and carry it out.'[v] [11] It is evident that no one is ever justified by observing the Law,[w] since it is written: 'Whoever is upright will live from (God's) fidelity.'

development, Paul celebrates the fidelity of God in history, not the subjective faith of believers.

s   Note, first, that the Torah remains an authority for Paul's 'gospel', and in fact had already proclaimed this gospel: secondly that Paul here expressly mentions the real theme of the letter: how the gentiles (not the Jews) arrive at justification.

t   In the preceding development, the emphasis is not on the faith of Abraham (as opposed to works), but to the fidelity of God. Abraham is not so much the model believer as the father of all gentiles justified through the fidelity of God.

u   In the stricter Jewish tradition, shared by Paul, pagans, even though outside the covenant, were obliged to carry out the demands of the Law, and were condemned for not doing so. Galatian Christians, who regarded certain practices of the Law as necessary for justification, were putting themselves outside the Christian economy of salvation and so stood condemned.

v   Judaisers did not observe the whole Law themselves and did not impose full observance on their followers. It is not a question here of the Law being impossible to observe perfectly. Observant Jews recognised this and found forgiveness for such shortcomings in the practice of their faith. It was one thing to fail to observe the whole Law perfectly and quite another to exempt oneself in principle from obedience to a number of its precepts.

w   Merely as a code, apart from the grace of the covenant.

¹² But the Law (as a code) is not based on (God's) fidelity; on the contrary, scripture says: 'The person who does these things will live by what he does.'[x] ¹³ Christ delivered us[y] from the curse of the Law by becoming himself for our sake an accursed thing; for scripture says: 'Cursed is everyone who is hanged on a tree.'[z] ¹⁴ The purpose of all this was to extend the blessing of Abraham to the gentiles in Christ Jesus, so that we,[a] by means of God's fidelity, might receive the promised Spirit.

Legal practice (3:15-18)

¹⁵ My brothers and sisters, let me put this in human terms. Even when a will is an ordinary human one, once it has been ratified, no one can cancel it or add provisions to it. ¹⁶ Now the promises were pronounced to Abraham 'and to his progeny'. The text does not say, 'and to his progenies' in the plural, but in the singular, 'and to his progeny', which means Christ.[b] ¹⁷ What I mean

---

x This is a very difficult text. Lev 18:15 is parallel to Hab 2:4 just cited: the verb 'live' in both texts is to be taken in the same sense. Thus the contrast between 3:12a and 3:12b is between the Law apart from the covenant (bringing a curse on pagans) and the Law with the covenant (based on God's fidelity) which brings life to those who fulfil it. Note the parallel in Lk 10:22: 'Do this and you will live.'

y Here Paul identifies himself with his gentile Christians

z The O.T. text is taken out of its context. In Deut 21:23, the person cursed is 'one guilty of a capital offence'. Jewish patriots crucified by Alexander Jannaeus would hardly be regarded as 'cursed'. Paul uses this text to put Jesus in solidarity with the gentiles as persons 'cursed' by the Law.

a See note v. 10.

b Paul used the singular 'progeny' to read a Christian meaning into the text: it is through Christ that the blessings of Abraham are to be granted to the pagans.

is this: a will had been already validated by God; it cannot be invalidated and its promise nullified by a Law made four hundred and thirty years later. [18] If the inheritance comes by the Law, then it no longer comes through a promise; but God bestowed it by a promise as a free gift to Abraham.[c]

The Law and the Gentiles (3:19-25)

[19] What then of the Law? It came on the scene to convict people of wrong-doing[d] until the 'progeny' to whom the promise had been made should come. It was promulgated through angels, and there was an intermediary. [20] The intermediary in question is not one of a kind. But God is one.[e]

---

c Paul in this text is thinking only of his pagan Christians. Abraham, justified by God's fidelity and his own faith and recipient of the promises, was, like the gentiles, without the Jewish Law and circumcision. Paul does not deny that the Jews who accept the Mosaic covenant and the Torah also inherit the promises. See Rom 3:29-30; 4:9; 9:4; 11:29. It is highly unlikely that Paul radically changed his views on the Law in the interval between his writing of Galatians and of Romans.

d Paul is here thinking of pagans. For the Jews, covenant and Torah went together, the Torah being the way of life God graciously called his people to follow. For the gentiles, the Law resulted in condemnation.

e To understand this difficult text, we must look at the Jewish tradition about the revelation of the Law to the gentiles and the place of the angels in God's government of them. Jewish tradition insisted that God spoke directly with his people at Sinai in the person of Moses. The contrast between the role of an intermediary and the one God seems to be in the setting of the promulgation of the Law to the gentiles. The various angels of the nations who communicated the Law to them were 'not of the one kind'. They were seventy different angels who could not represent the one God; and they were limited to their role of keeping the nations in slavery. The one God

21 Does the Law then contradict the promises? Not at all! If a Law had been given that could bestow life, then in fact saving justice would come from the Law. 22 But scripture has declared the whole world prisoners under sin, so that the promised blessing should be given through the fidelity of Jesus Christ to all those who believe.

23 Before this fidelity was enacted, we*f* were prisoners in custody of the Law awaiting the revelation of God's fidelity, 24 so that the Law was a sort of slave in charge of children, until Christ should come and we could be justified from God's fidelity. 25 Now that this fidelity has arrived, we are no longer under the charge of a slave.

Christian tradition (3:26 – 4:11)

26 Through this fidelity you are all children of God in Christ Jesus. 27 Baptised into union with him, you have all put on Christ as a garment. 28 There is no such thing any more as Jew and Greek, slave and free, male or female: you are all one person in Christ Jesus.*g* 29 But, if you belong to Christ, you are the 'progeny' of Abraham, and heirs by promise.

spoke directly to Israel: Moses here is not an intermediary, but identified with Israel. The theme of the 'one God' is used elsewhere
in Paul to indicate the opening up of salvation to the pagans (Rom
3:29-30).

f   This refers in fact to the gentiles, with whom Paul identifies himself.
g   Paul is thinking of his communities of pagan converts to which he
and other Jewish missionaries belonged. Perhaps the best commentary on this text is Eph 2:11-18, where the pagan Christians are
reminded of the time when they were 'excluded from membership
of Israel, aliens with no part in the covenant of the promises, limited
to this world, without hope and without God'. Now the Law as
a dividing force is abolished and in the Christian community pagans
are called to be 'fellow citizens of the holy people of God and part
of God's household'.

4 ¹ Speaking of heirs, I remind you that as long as the heir is a minor he is no better off than a slave, even though he is the owner of all the property; ² he is under guardians and trustees until the time fixed by his father. ³ So we,*ʰ* when we were minors, were slaves to the elemental spirits of the universe.*ⁱ* ⁴ When the appointed time finally came, God sent his Son, born of a woman, born under the Law,*ʲ* ⁵ to liberate those who were under the Law, so that we*ᵏ* might attain to the status of children. ⁶ Because you are children, God has sent the Spirit of his Son into your hearts crying 'Abba! Father!' ⁷ You are therefore no longer a slave but a child, and if a child, then also by God's very act an heir.

⁸ Formerly, when you did not acknowledge God, you were the slaves of things called gods, who are no gods

---

h   The gentiles, with whom Paul identifies himself.

i   These 'elemental spirits' are later (4:8) identified with false gods. Such a situation clearly refers not to Jews but to gentiles. Another view, which would hold that, according to Paul, the Law was in fact given, not by God, but by demonic spirits to lead the people of Israel to disaster, is hardly tenable. It would mean a rejection of Judaism so total and absolute as to exclude all faith and grace from Israel from the time of Moses to the time of Jesus. Besides being in contradiction with Romans (written shortly after Galatians), it is contradicted by Paul's own acceptance of the Torah as divinely inspired, for the Torah gives clear witness to the living faith of Israel.

j   If Paul had wished to say that Jesus was made subject to the Law by circumcision, he could have said so clearly. As it is, he begins by situating Jesus at birth in solidarity with all human beings as one 'born of a woman'. The same verb *genomenon* is used in the phrase 'born under the Law' and should have the same meaning. Thus, before being incorporated into the people of Israel by circumcision, Jesus shared the lot of the gentiles as one 'under the Law'. Abraham too was the recipient of God's promises before circumcision.

k   As before, Paul uses 'we' here of the pagans. This is made clear by the change to 'you' in the following development.

at all.*l* *9* But now that you do acknowledge God — or rather that now God has acknowledged you — how can you turn back to the mean and beggarly elemental spirits, how can you wish to enter their service all over again?*m* *10* You observe special days and months and seasons and years.*n* *11* You make me fear that all the labour I spent on you has been in vain.

Friendship (4:12-20)

12 My brothers and sisters, put yourself in my place, since I have put myself in yours. You have never wronged me. *13* As you know, it was an illness that first gave me the opportunity of preaching the gospel to you, *14* and you overcame any temptation to show scorn or disgust. On the contrary, you welcomed me as if I were an angel from heaven, as you might have welcomed Christ Jesus himself. *15* What has happened to that happy relationship? I can testify that at that time you would have willingly torn out your eyes and given them to me, if that were possible! *16* To think that I have now made myself your enemy by telling you the truth!

17 These other people are courting you, but to no good end. They really want to cut you off from me, so that you

---

l   The slavery to 'things called gods' is the equivalent of the slavery to the cosmic powers mentioned above in 4:3.

m   To be 'under the Law' is the same as being condemned by the Law. Without Christ, such people return to slavery under these elemental spirits. It is clear that, in both cases, we are dealing with gentiles, not Jews. In no way could Judaism be ever regarded as a service of false gods.

n   These, no doubt, are some of the observances of the Law selected by the Judaisers. See 3:10; 5:3.

may court them. [18] It is a fine thing to court another's following in a worthy cause — and this applies to our relationship at all times, and not only when I am present with you. [19] My dear children, I am going through the pain of giving birth to you all over again, until Christ takes shape in you. [20] I wish I could be with you at this moment; then I could change the way I talk. I really don't know how to deal with you.

Allegory from Scripture (4:21-31)[o]

[21] Tell me, then, you who are so eager to be under the Law, why don't you listen to what the Law says?[p] [22] It is written there that Abraham had two sons, one by his slave and one by his free-born wife. [23] The slave-woman's son was born in the way of nature, the free woman's was born through a promise. [24] This is an allegory. The two women stand for two covenants.[q] The first covenant comes from Sinai and leads into slavery: [25] that is Hagar.

---

o   This text is commonly presented as Paul's sharpest attack on his own people, whom in Rom 9:1-3 he professes to love so much! Particularly the words of Sarah (Gen 21:10): 'Drive out the slave-woman and her child,' applied here by Paul to Israel, have been echoed by Christians through the centuries as they persecuted the people of Jesus. In recent times another interpretation of the text has been offered, which is followed here.

p   The Torah as teaching remains valid for all Christians. Paul constantly cites it, not merely in its Christian application (as here) but also in its literal sense (e.g. Gen 2:24 in 1 Cor 6:16).

q   These two covenants do not indicate the 'old' and the 'new' covenants of Christian tradition, but the two covenants, those God made with Israel and with Hagar together with her offspring (Gen 21:17-21). Hagar and her people are associated with the desert, in which, according to Jewish tradition, the Law was offered to them from Sinai and refused.

Sinai is a mountain in Arabia.[r] Hagar stands in contrast[s] with the Jerusalem of today, for she is enslaved with her children. [26] But the Jerusalem above is a free woman and she is our mother, [27] for scripture says, 'Rejoice, you barren woman, who never bore a child; break into shouts of joy, you have never known 'a mother's pangs; for the deserted wife shall have more children than she who lives with a husband.'[t]

[28] And you, my brothers and sisters, are children of the promise, like Isaac. [29] But, just as in those days the natural-born son persecuted the spiritual son, so now.[u] [30] But what does scripture say? 'Drive out the slave-woman and her son, for the son of the slave shall not share the inheritance with the sons of the free woman.' [31] You see, brothers and sisters, we are children not of the slave-woman; our mother is the free woman.

5 [1] Christ set us free, to remain free people. Stand firm, then, and refuse to be tied to the yoke of slavery again.[v]

---

r Arabia was the territory of Hagar's offspring. Paul, in a rather forced way, links the giving of the Law on Sinai with its proclamation to pagan nations (including the children of Hagar) and their refusal to accept it. This was a common theme in Jewish tradition.

s This is much more likely the meaning of *systoichei*.

t Io 54:1. Note that in Is 54:11-17 the thought moves from the 'present Jerusalem' to the 'Jerusalem above'. The continuity between Israel and the Christian church is also celebrated by Paul in the image of the olive tree in Rom 11:16-24.

u Gentile Christians share the promises made to Israel (Rom 3:29-30; 4:16; 11:16-24). The Judaisers, who harass them and try to force them into subjection to the Law are themselves slaves to the Law and trying to bring the Galatians into the same slavery.

v This conclusion shows that the adversaries who are trying to lead the gentile Christians into slavery are not Jews, but (probably

EXHORTATION (5:1 – 6:10)

2 Mark my words: I, Paul, tell you that if you receive circumcision Christ will be of no benefit to you whatsoever.
3 Once again you can take it from me that every one who receives circumcision is bound to keep the whole Law.*w*
4 When you seek to be justified by way of the Law, you have separated yourself from Christ, you have fallen from grace. 5 For to us, our hope of attaining the saving justice we await is the work of the Spirit through faith. 6 For in Christ Jesus what is important is not circumcision or the lack of it, but faith which is active in love. 7 For a while you were running well. Who was it hindered you from following the truth? 8 The argument used to persuade you did not come from the one who called you.
9 Just a tiny bit of yeast leavens all the dough. 10 United with you in the Lord I am convinced that you will not take a wrong view. The person who is disturbing you, such a person must bear God's judgment. 11 And I, brothers and sisters, if I am still preaching circumcision,*x* why am I still being persecuted? In that case, my preaching

---

gentile) Christian Judaisers. From this background the 'allegory' is to be understood.

w The Judaisers do not keep the whole Law themselves (6:13) and are pagan converts. It is highly unlikely that zealous Jews would on principle observe only some of the precepts of the Law. The point here is not that every single detail of the Torah had to be observed by the Jews for salvation: they give every evidence of their belief in a merciful and forgiving God. The Judaisers were making a selection from the Law, and leaving out other precepts. Paul insists that the Law cannot be treated in this piece-meal way.

x This probably refers to Paul's pre-Christian days. His concern for the salvation of the gentiles, even before his meeting with the risen Lord, seems to have led him to engage in a proselytising campaign, in which he took the narrower Jewish view that, for salvation, gentiles had to become Jews and so receive circumcision.

of the cross would no longer be a stumbling block. 12 As for the people who are disturbing you, why don't they go the whole way and castrate themselves?

13 My brothers and sisters, you were called to freedom. Only do not turn your freedom into an occasion for indulging human nature, but be servants to one another in love. 14 For the whole of the Law can be summed up in one commandment: 'You shall love your neighbour as yourself.'*y* 15 But if you go on snapping and snarling at one another, all you can expect is mutual destruction.

16 What I mean is this: if you are guided by the Spirit, you will not carry out purely human of our lower nature. 17 That nature sets its desires against the Spirit, and the desires of the Spirit are against nature. For these two are opposed to one another, so that you find yourselves unable to do the things you want to do. 18 But if you are led by the Spirit, you are not subject to any code of Law.*z*

19 Our lower nature reveals itself in its behaviour: fornication, impurity, and indecency, 20 idolatry and sorcery; quarrels, rivalry, outbursts of anger, selfish ambitions, dissension, 21 factions; drinking bouts, orgies, and the like. I warn you now as I warned you before, 22 that people who behave in these ways will not inherit the kingdom of God.

22 But the fruit of the Spirit is love, joy, peace, patience, kindness, goodness, fidelity, 23 gentleness and self-control: these things go beyond any code of Law. 24 All

---

y Paul here is in the line of Jesus (Mt 22:34-40) and of the Jewish tradition which saw the Law summed up in one's relationship with one's neighbour.

z We have already seen that the term 'under the Law' refers to the situation of gentiles, not of Jews. For gentiles outside the covenant the Torah of the Jews became a code of Law.

who belong to Christ Jesus have crucified their lower nature with its passions and desires. 25 Since we live by the Spirit, let our behaviour be guided by the Spirit. 26 We must not be conceited, provocative and jealous of one another.

6 1 My brothers and sisters, if one of you is caught do- ing something wrong, you who are gifted with the Spirit should set such a person right in a spirit of gentle- ness. Look to yourselves, each one of you: you may be tempted too. 2 Bear one another's burdens: in this way you will fulfil the Law of Christ.

3 People who think themselves important are simply deceiving themselves. 4 We should all examine our own conduct; we should limit ourselves to esteeming our own achievements,*a* without making comparisons with other people. 5 We all have our own burdens to bear.

6 When anyone is under instruction in the faith, such a person should give the teacher a share in all his goods.

7 Make no mistake: God is not to be fooled. You reap what you sow. 8 If you sow seed in the field of your lower nature, you will reap from it a harvest of corruption. But if you sow in the field of the Spirit, the Spirit will bring you a harvest of eternal life. 9 We should never grow weary of doing good, for if we do not slacken our efforts, we shall in due time reap our harvest.*b* 10 So, according

---

a Paul has no problem with the Christian's assessment of his own 'work'. In this, he is not so far removed from the religious rabbi. Both see works as a necessary and required consequence of genuine faith.

b Another example of 'works' and reward in Pauline theology.

to our opportunity, let us work for the good of all, especially members of the household of the faith.

CONCLUSION (6:11-18)

[11] You see these big letters? I am writing to you now with my own hand. [12] People who want to cut a good figure by human standards, these are the people who are forcing circumcision on you. Their only reason is to avoid persecution for the cross of Christ. [13] For though they accept circumcision,[c] they do not themselves observe the Law; they want you to be circumcised, only that they may boast of your human subjection. [14] As for me, I have no desire to boast, except in the cross of our Lord, Jesus Christ, through whom the world has been crucified to me and I to the world. [15] Circumcision does not matter; neither does lack of circumcision. The only thing which matters is a new creation. [16] Peace and mercy on all who follow this rule of life and on the Israel of God.[d]

[17] In future, let no one trouble me, for I bear the marks of Jesus branded on my body.

[18] The grace of our Lord Jesus Christ, brothers and sisters, be with your spirit. Amen.

---

c The present participle points to gentile Christians rather than to Jews. Also the fact that they do not observe the Law indicates that they are gentiles, not Jews.

d The more normal meaning of this phrase would indicate the historical people of Israel. The more commonly accepted interpretation of Galatians would hardly allow this meaning, whereas it fits in quite well with the general interpretation given above. The main point of Paul's argument is that the pagans through the fidelity of Christ share the blessings of the people of Israel.